UGLY BUGS ACTIVITY BOOK

Nick Arnold ✹ Tony De Saulles

"Ugly bugs are experts at hiding from larger beasts that might try to eat them. Some blend in with their surroundings, others look like something else. A stick insect looks like a stick and a Japanese leaf insect looks like ... well, what do you think? There are FIVE speckled moths to spot in this book — can you find them all?"

SCHOLASTIC

IT'S A BUG'S LIFE!

Ugly bugs come in all shapes and sizes – there are insects with six legs and spiders with eight. There are worms with no legs and millipedes with … er, lots! But they've all got one thing in common – they're ugly! And their horrible habits are even worse. Here's our bug boffin, Craig Cutting, to talk us through the foul facts.

OH, NO! This poor little beetle's had a horrible accident! Can you add the stickers for the missing parts?

EYES
Used for spotting anything that moves that is worth eating

WING
Used f...

REAR BODY
The guts are in here

FEE...
Used for touchi... and sniffing

SKIN
Light, water-proof and tough

...ve thre... ointed pairs

Insects I love 'em all — but some of them are a bit antisocial. Can you add the bug stickers to this wanted poster?

If an ugly bug has got more than six legs, or no legs at all, it isn't an insect. So that includes nasties like slugs, woodlice, spiders and of course, worms. See if you can untangle this slimy wriggling mess to find out which earthworm is going to have its head bitten off by the hungry mole.

WANTED:
THE UGLY BUG GANG

1 Clue: pinch, pinch

Earwig
Said to crawl into your ear when you're asleep. Beware, its rear-end pincers!

2 Clue: yum yum

Biscuit beetle
Steals and scoffs your digestive biscuits (but not the chocolate ones).

3 Clue: squirt

Ladybird
Produces stinky liquid when it's upset, and it can even bite.

4 Clue: slurp, slurp

Bug
Sucks vegetable juices through its straw-like mouth. Some like a drop of blood.

5 Clue: lick, lick

Fly
Likes to lick the top of a big smelly cowpat — then pay a visit to whatever you're going to eat.

6 Clue: glup

Lice
It lives on other creatures so it can suck a drop of blood whenever it likes!

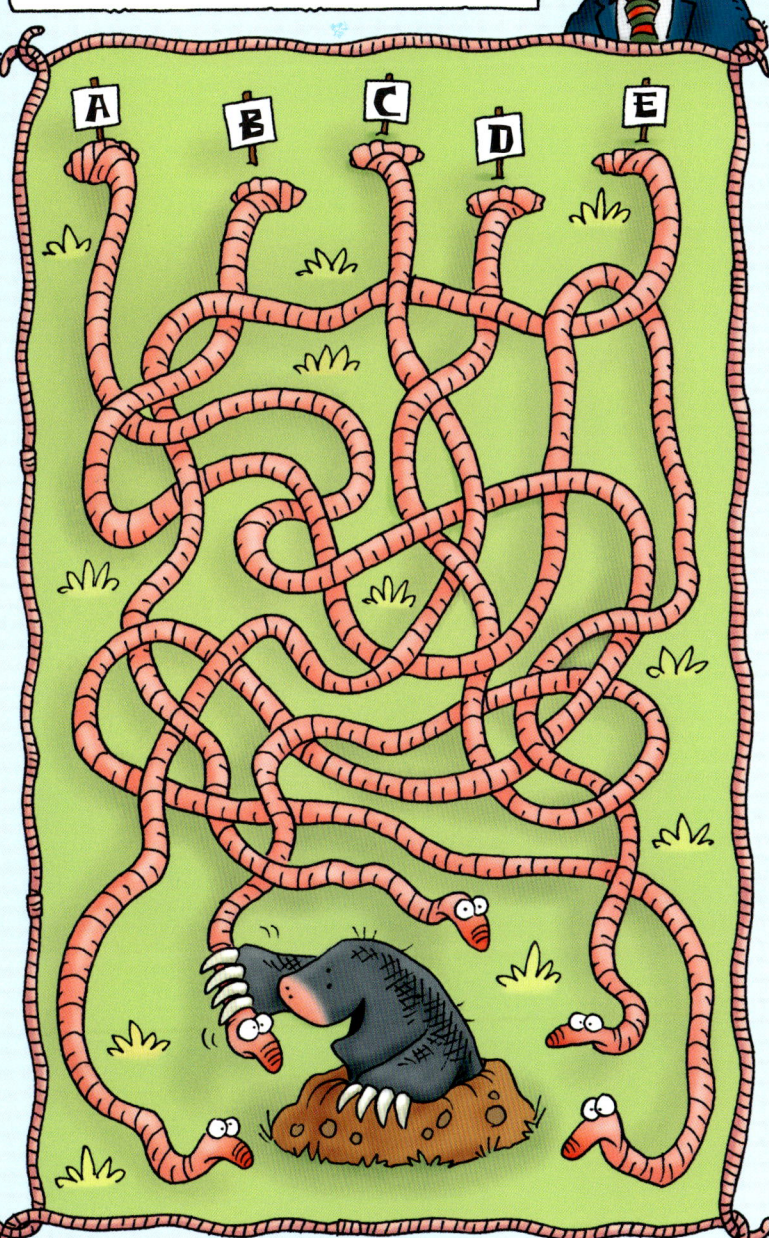

BET YOU NEVER KNEW...
Salted and fried woodlice are an African speciality. They eat them like crisps!

PRETTY UGLIES AND SLEAZY BEES

It's easy to tell a butterfly from a bee. Butterflies look pretty, but start off as ugly caterpillars. Bees make us honey, but carry an ugly sting in their tails. Now read on for more pretty sleazy facts.

It's a risky business being a juicy caterpillar, as there's always the chance that you'll be scoffed by a larger creature. Luckily, they've mastered the cunning trick of camouflage — disguising their body to blend in with their surroundings. Add the stickers to complete the picture. Now take a close look and see how many crawling caterpillars you can find hiding. Can you spot the hawk moth caterpillar? Its rear end looks like a snake's head.

The large blue butterfly is — amazingly enough, a large blue butterfly! In Britain it is very rare and is currently only found in a few places in the West Country. Add the stickers to complete the picture. Copy the lines in each square onto the empty grid and colour it in.

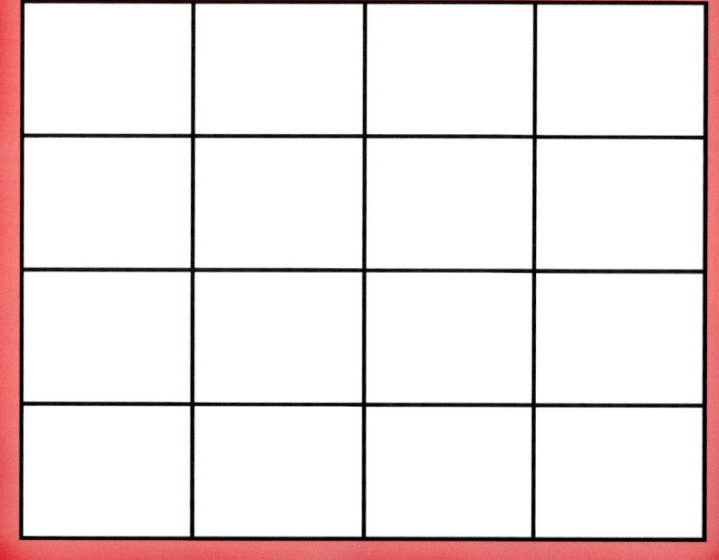

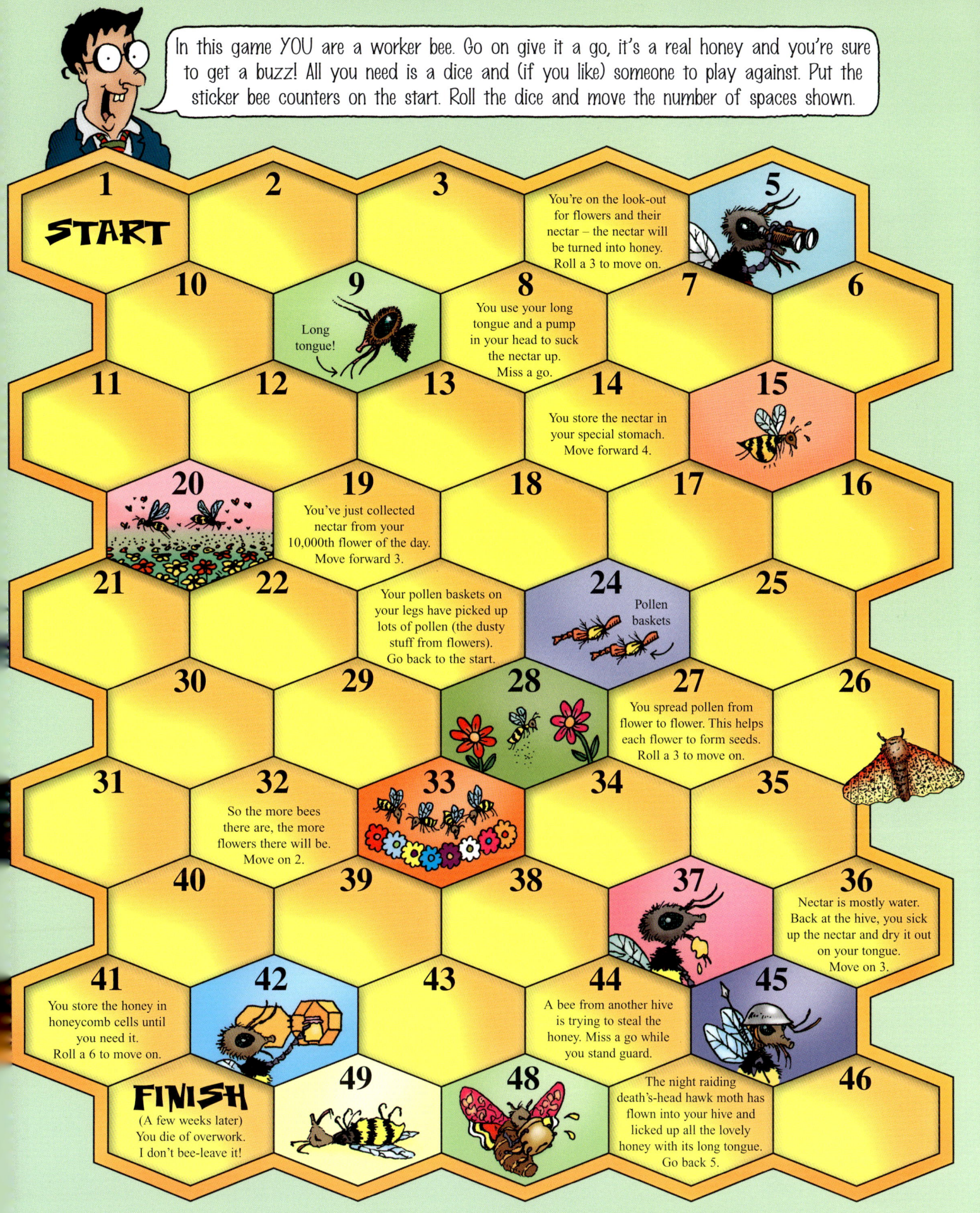

AWFULLY AWESOME ANTS

Ants can be pretty awful, they get everywhere from your plants to your pants.
But they can be pretty awesome, too, in all sorts of horrible ways.

Bet you didn't know that marauder ants build their own roads, which can be as long as 90 metres, and if you're ant-sized, that's awesome! The ants have to follow a strict highway code. Find the stickers to fill in the missing words and discover who has the right of way and who's likely to end up in a crazy creepy-crawly crash!

The Marauder Ants' Highway Code

Always keep to your own part of the ☐ . Returning ants in the ☐ , outwards ants at the ☐ .

Move anything that gets in your ☐ . If it's ☐ , gnaw it.

If it's ☐ , get the younger ants to ☐ it off the road.

If you can eat it, bring it back to the ☐ — 100 workers can shift one ☐ , 30 workers can shift one ☐ .

If you cross any other ant roads ... ☐ the other ants!

All ugly bugs that get in the way must be ☐ alive!

WHAT'S HAPPENING?

CAN WE TALK ABOUT THIS?

Help the weary worker ant find his way through the maze and out into the sunny garden for a well-deserved rest. But watch out for the quarrelsome queen ant, if she catches you trying to sneak out of the nest, she'll send you right back to the beginning of the maze.

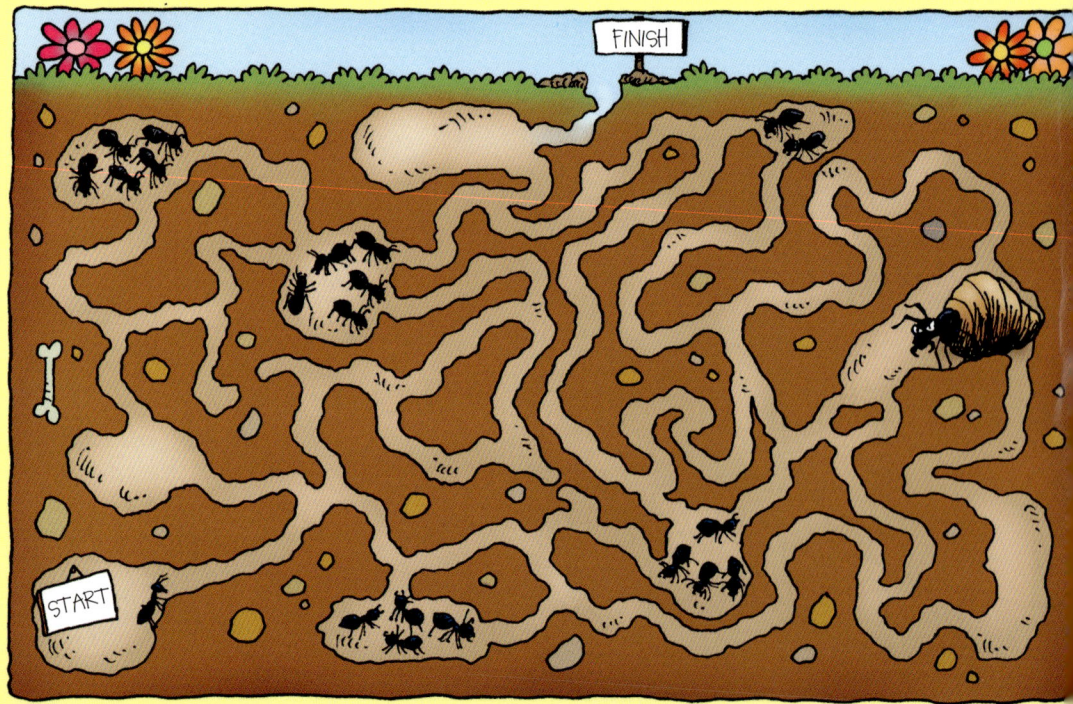

Stickers for INSIDE FRONT COVER

SPARE STICKERS

Stickers for INSIDE BACK COVER

SPARE STICKERS

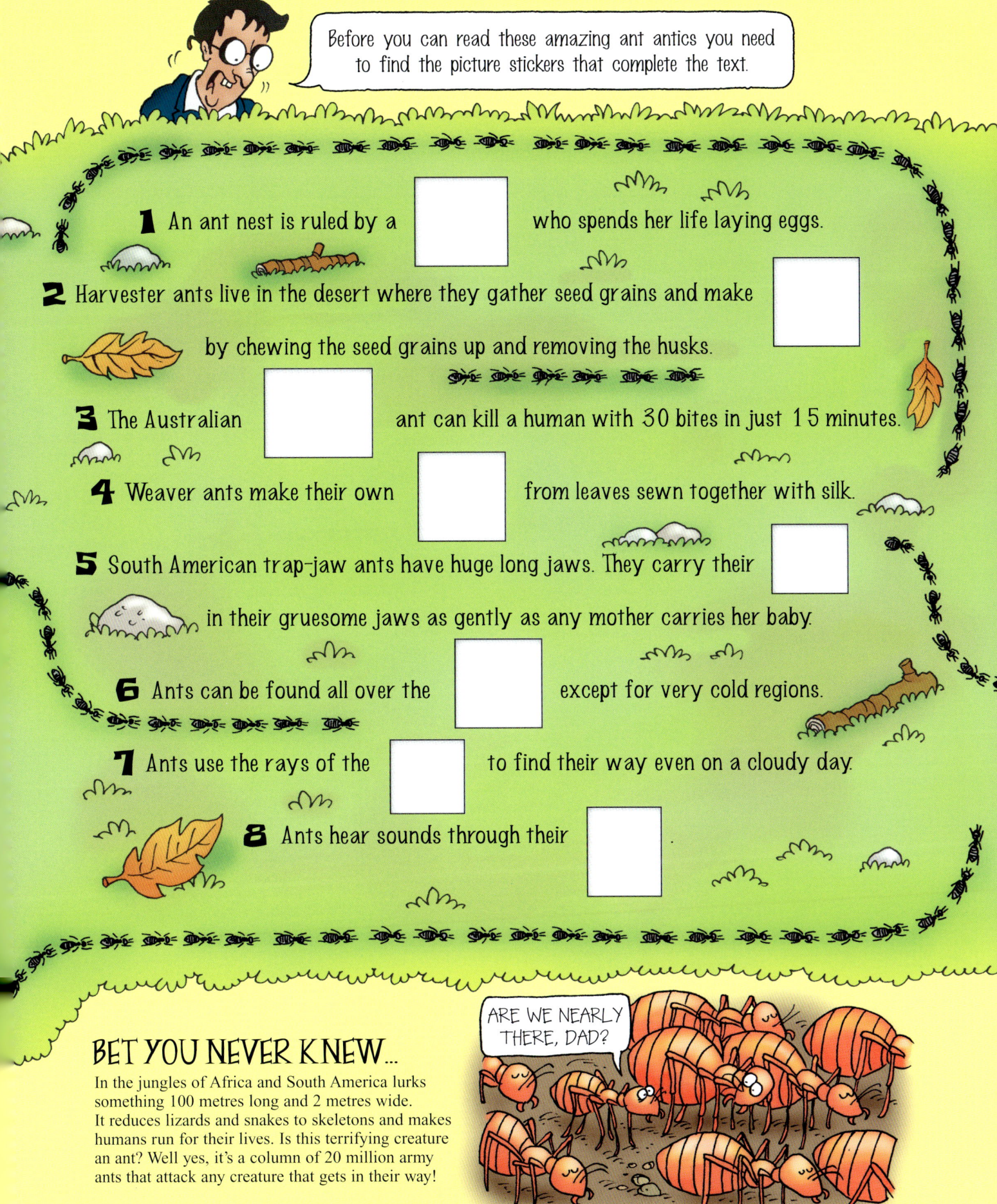

UGLY BUG WATER WORLD RESORT

Why not relax by a peaceful pond or river and forget about those horrible ugly bugs? Some chance! Ugly bugs like water even more than you do. Grab your swimming costume and join in the fun. Just watch out for the bugs!

Let's meet the residents of this low-life pond resort. Read the clues and see if you can find the stickers to match the ugly bug to its loathsome lifestyle.

THE POND RESORT

a) Water scorpion
Hangs under the water and grabs passing bugs in its claws and sucks out their juices.

b) Water measurer
Walks around on the surface of the pond looking for bugs that have fallen in.

c) Whirligig beetle
Has four eyes — one pair above the water and one pair below.

e) Great pond snail
Hangs upside down from the surface of the pond and stores air in its shell.

d) Water flea
Lives in the water and leaps to escape.

f) Water spider
Lives in an underwater diving bell made from silk and air bubbles.

SERIOUSLY SAVAGE SPIDERS

Spiders aren't insects – for one thing they have an extra pair of legs. But more people are scared of spiders than of insects. I wonder why?

Here's a little quiz to find out how much you know about spiders' seriously savage habits. Use a pencil to circle the answer you think is correct.

1. How does a spider attack its prey?
a) It scares them to death.
b) It smothers them in a silky web.
c) It paralyses them with poison fangs and sucks out the juices.

2. How do spiders avoid getting caught in their own webs?
a) By their nifty footwork.
b) They have oily non-stick feet.
c) They slide down a line and pulley.

3. What does a spider do with its old web?
a) It wears them.
b) It throws them away.
c) It eats them.

EIGHT WALKING STICKS – HE MUST BE OLD!

4. What is the black widow spider famous for eating?
a) Her babies.
b) Her husband.
c) Herself.

WHAT'S FOR PUDDING?

5. When a spider sheds its skin what part does it get rid of?
a) Its skin.
b) The front of its eyes.
c) The lining of its guts and book lung (the bit a spider breathes through).

6. What particularly horrible habit does the house spider have?
a) It spits out bits of insect and leaves them lying around for someone else to tidy up.
b) It poos in the bath.
c) It spins webs in your hair.

7. What does a spitting spider do?
a) It spits a poison that kills its victims as they try to escape.
b) It lassoes its victims with a 10-cm squirt of silk that ties them to the ground.
c) Nothing. It sits around looking strangely sinister.

8. What, according to legend, is the best way to cure the bite of a tarantula spider?
a) A cup of tea.
b) A lively folk dance.
c) Suck out the venom.

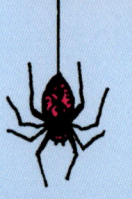

Dare you make friends with a spider? To save spinning your own silk, try asking a spider to make some for you.

We've all heard the rhyme about little Miss Muffet who got scared away by a great big spider. But there was a real Miss Patience Mouffet, who was the daughter of sixteenth-century spider scientist, Dr Thomas Mouffet. Her dad used to dose her up with live spiders whenever she had a cold. Find the stickers to complete the picture, and then see if you can spot the ten differences.

DARE YOU DISCOVER

1) Cut a plastic lemonade bottle in half.

2) Add soil and twigs to the bottom half.

3) Now find your spider — sheds and out-houses are good places to look. If you find a web, the spider is normally nearby. One spider is enough. Add two and one will eat the other! Be gentle — spiders are easily hurt!

4) Tape up the two halves of the bottle.

5) Feed your new friend with a small fly through the top of the bottle.

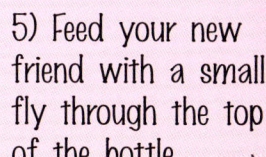

6) See if she's spun any silk or made a web. If she has, try knitting some spider-silk gloves. Don't forget to free her when you've finished.

BET YOU NEVER KNEW...

The trap-door spider digs a tunnel with a trap door at one end. The spider waits inside the tunnel. It grabs a passing insect and pulls it down. The door closes and the innocent victim is never seen again.

SHUT THE DOOR — THERE'S A TERRIBLE DRAUGHT COMING DOWN THE TUNNEL!

ANSWER PAGE
IT'S A BUG'S LIFE!
OH, NO! This poor little beetle's...

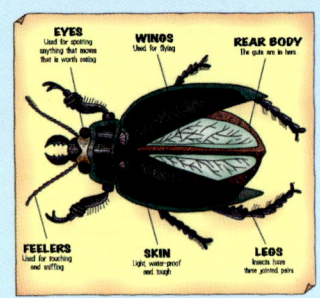

Insects I love 'em all – but some...

Earwig = d   Biscuit beetle = a   Ladybird = b
Bug = c   Fly = f   Lice = e

If an ugly bug has got more...
Earthworm D is going to get his head bitten off!

PRETTY UGLIES AND SLEAZY BEES
It's a risky business being...
There are 35 crawling caterpillars hiding in the bush. The hawk moth caterpillar is ringed.

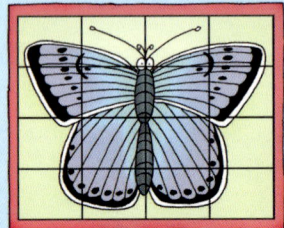

The large blue butterfly is – amazingly...

AWFULLY AWESOME ANTS
Bet you didn't know that marauder ants...

Missing words in the correct order: ROAD, MIDDLE, EDGES, WAY, BIG, SMALL, CARRY, NEST, EARTHWORM, SEED, KILL, EATEN.

Help the weary worker...

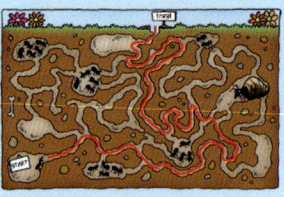

Before you can read these amazing ant...
Missing pictures in the correct order...

UGLY BUG WATER WORLD RESORT
Let's meet the residents of this low-life...

a) 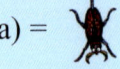   b)    c)
d)   e)    f)

Ready for some action? Then pop into...
Boating beetles B and D are the same.

Lurking at the bottom of the resort are...
MONDAY: Leech climbs to the top of its jar means that rain is expected. TUESDAY: Lazy leech lies on the bottom of his jar means fine or frosty weather. WEDNESDAY: A restless leech shows that a storm is on its way.

SERIOUSLY SAVAGE SPIDERS
Here's a little quiz to find out how...

1. = c   2. = b   3. = c   4. = b
5. = a/b/c   6. = a   7. = b   8. = b

We've all heard the rhyme about little...

The speckled moths can be found in the *Wanted: The Ugly Bug Gang*, the *board game*, *The Marauder Ants' Highway Code*, *The Pond Resort* and on the *Dare you Discover* activities

---

Scholastic Children's Books,
Euston House, 24 Eversholt Street,
London NW1 1DB, UK
A division of Scholastic Ltd
London ~ New York ~ Toronto ~ Auckland ~
Sydney ~ Mexico City ~ New Delhi ~ Hong Kong
Published in the UK by Scholastic Ltd, 2006
Some of the material in this book has previously been published in Horrible Science:
Ugly Bugs

Text copyright © Nick Arnold, 1996
Illustrations copyright © Tony De Saulles, 1996
All rights reserved
ISBN 0 439 95579 3
13 digit ISBN 978 0 439 95579 9
2 4 6 8 10 9 7 5 3 1

The right of Nick Arnold and Tony De Saulles to be identified as the author and illustrator of this work respectively has been asserted by them in accordance with the Copyright, Designs and Patents Act, 1988.

Additional material by Dereen Taylor
Additional illustrations and colour work by
Mike Phillips and Stuart Martin

Created and produced by The Complete Works,
St Mary's Road, Royal Leamington Spa,
Warwickshire CV31 1JP, UK

Printed and bound
by Tien Wah Press Pte. Ltd, Malaysia

This book is sold subject to the condition that it shall not, by way of trade or otherwise be lent, resold, hired out, or otherwise circulated without the publisher's prior consent in any form of binding or cover other than that in which it is published and without a similar condition, including this condition, being imposed on a subsequent purchaser.